A Beginner's Guide To
Guinea Pigs

Written By
Tom Willkie

Introduction

A rodent, the Guinea Pig is closely related to the mouse and hamster—certainly more closely related to those other rodents than to the pig. He is also called a Cavy.

There is considerable speculation as to how he acquired the name "Guinea Pig," because he didn't come from the West African coast of Guinea or from New Guinea in the South Pacific. Nor is he a pig.

One explanation for the name "guinea" is that he was sold in England for a guinea (an old English coin no longer minted). Another version is that the ships carrying the Cavies from South America came by way of the West African coast of Guinea. This may have led the people to believe that they came from Guinea instead of South America, thereby attributing that name to the animal. The last and most logical reason is that many Cavies were exported from Guiana in South America, and because of the similarity between Guiana and Guinea, people may have confused the two and pronounced the more familiar Guinea.

The name "pig" is little more understandable and entirely unjust. The Cavy has the habit of squealing, grunting or squeaking when hungry, excited or afraid. This is as far as the similarity between the Cavy and the pig goes. While the pig seemingly enjoys wallowing in dirt and filth, the Cavy is perhaps the cleanest animal in the world. To further confuse the problem, male Cavies are correctly referred to as "boars," while the females

Regardless of by which name it is known, the Cavy is an inoffensive and appealing animal. Photo by Louise Van der Meid.

are designated "sows." Since it is now obvious that the Cavy was misnamed "Guinea Pig" we will, in the future, refer to him as "*Cavy.*"

Since Cavies are small, relatively little space is needed to house them. They require little care and attention to keep them healthy and happy.

Because of their size and ease of care it is just as easy (up to a point, of course) to have many Cavies as it is to have one. Cavies are usually kept in pairs or in families of one male and two or more females.

Compared with other small rodents they don't breed as often, and their litters are considerably smaller.

If cared for properly they contract few diseases, if any. Cavies have a long life span, averaging over seven years.

Cavies offer almost limitless possibilities for variation of color and hair.

Cavies seldom bite and have a gentle and friendly disposition. When kept clean Cavies are odorless.

These qualities together with his charming features and a special human appeal have made the Cavy one of our most popular small pets.

A Cavy is capable of showing curiosity about its surroundings. Photo by Michael Gilroy.

1.
History

The Cavy is believed to be one of the earliest animals domesticated by man. Remains of the Cavy have been found buried along with the mummies in the tombs of the Incas.

Cavies have been man's pets for a long time, but most of the different color varieties available today are relatively recent developments. Photo by Michael Gilroy.

Ancestors of our present domesticated Cavies originated in Peru. They were domesticated in great numbers by the Indians of Peru, Colombia and Ecuador long before the arrival of the Spanish in the sixteenth century. The Indians kept the Cavy for its meat, which was highly prized. Cavies were first introduced into Europe by the Spaniards returning from their conquests in South America. Soon after, the Cavy found its way to North America and today is found in abundance in all parts of the world.

The Cavy has received much attention in the exhibition hall.

The Cavy has rendered a great service to mankind, but is no longer used to as great a degree because of the simple fact that they don't produce enough offspring. Hamsters, mice and rabbits have largely taken over the role of the Cavy in the laboratory because they produce astronomically. For example, in 12 months the mouse can theoretically produce 5,000 times as many offspring as the Cavy.

Due to his retirement from the field of research, the Cavy is now left with the sole responsibility of providing many people with pleasure either as a pet or as a breeding hobby.

Description

Your full grown Cavy (from the age of six months and up) will weigh 34 to 42 oz. and be 10 in. long, although there is some variation in size. The boar will be slightly

Cavies can be enjoyed by anyone—all you have to give them is affection and good care.

The comparatively large head and the four toes on the front feet are easily visible even in this one-day-old Cavy. Photo by Michael Gilroy.

larger than the unbred sow. Your Cavy will have a short stocky body, short legs, large head, blunt nose, and short, naked, rounded ears. His fore limbs have four toes, and the hind limbs have three toes. All the toes are equipped with broad claws.

An interesting characteristic of the Cavy is that he has no external tail, but has retained an internal tail. One of the standard jokes of Cavy breeders is to tell a beginner, "Pick a Cavy up by the tail and his eyes fall out." The victim looks quite sheepish when he can't find a tail.

2.
Varieties

Of the various breeds of Cavies, the distinguishing characteristics are mainly in the length and texture of the hair which varies from very harsh and rough to a very luxurious silky smooth coat. The length varies from a short-cropped coat to a long-flowing coat.

Shown above is an orange and white female Cavy. A number of different colors and hair types are available. Photo by Michael Gilroy.

Richly colored and very attractive, this is an American Crested Cavy. Photo by Brian Seed.

This variation in length and texture of the coat provides the best means of classifying the various breeds. The three possible combinations of hair characteristics produce the three hair classifications.

Long hair

Smooth hair: Angora or Peruvian.

Short hair

Smooth hair: English or Bolivian.
Rough hair: Abyssinian.

Hair color is another characteristic which is often used as a means of classification. The colors include black, tan, cream, chocolate, red, white, golden, silver, blue,

The rough hair of the Abyssinian Cavy is illustrated here. Photo by Brian Seed.

cinnamon, orange, beige, lilac and slate. In addition to these solid colors, there are unlimited possibilities for combinations of colors and patterns.

In order to better acquaint you with the wide selection of colors and the various varieties, it will be good to take a closer look at some of the more popular types of Cavies. It is this vast selection of breed and color that makes it possible for everyone to exercise his own personal taste when choosing his pet.

English or Bolivian

This is the popular short-haired variety, available in every Cavy color and combination of colors. It is the variety most commonly kept as a pet.

Abyssinian

Distinguished from the other varieties by his ruffled fur which forms rosettes. His fur is similar to that of a wire terrier.

Peruvian

The Peruvian is one of the oldest and scarcest varieties of Cavy. His fur should consist of long, fine silky hair growing on all parts of the body. The coat should part from the spine and flow down the sides like a mane. It should be of such even length that at a glance it should be difficult to determine which is the head and which is the tail.

The color is of little importance in contributing to the beauty of the Peruvian. The most popular colors are black, red, white, orange, cream and slate. The length of the coat is the most important factor in his beauty. In fact, the longer the better. The Peruvian is to the

This black Himalayan Cavy shows good nose-area markings. Photo by Brian Seed.

Cavy as the Palomino is to the horse. Here is the aristocrat of the Cavies.

Agouti

The Agouti is given credit as being the basis of all other varieties. It is said to be the original animal brought back from South America by the Spanish.

There are two distinct varieties, the Silver Agouti and the Golden Agouti. The marking is a mixture of black-

and-silver or black-and-gold, the black forming the base of the hairs with the tops of silver or gold. The silver Agouti should have a rich silver coat with a pale silver belly. The Golden Agouti should have a rich golden coat with a rich mahogany belly.

"Self"

"Self" is the term applied to the solid-colored coat. It is this type that is the most popular and in greatest demand. There are two reasons for its popularity: (1) it is not as difficult to produce the solid colors, and (2) in breeding, its shade, size, shape and coat can be more easily controlled than other types.

The distinctive features of the "Self" Cavy are that it is large in size, has a short cobby body, deep shoulders, and a short blunt Roman nose. The eyes are large, bold and well set. The ears are even and drooping in the shape of rose petals. There are seven colors in the "Self" Cavy: black, white, chocolate, red, lilac, beige and cream. Whites are by far the most popular. Through years of careful breeding the colors have reached a point of perfection in purity, brightness and richness of tone.

Dutch

The Dutch Cavy's name is derived from the similarity of its markings to the Dutch Rabbit. Dutch Cavies are known to exist in five recognized colors: red, black, agouti, chocolate and silver agouti. These colors mark the cheeks, ears and hindquarters, but all have an underlying background of white which forms a kind of saddle and strip down the front of the face.

A Dalmatian Cavy, one of the rarer color varieties.
Photo by Brian Seed.

Because this particular variety is rather difficult to breed true to pattern the demand far exceeds the supply. The distinct markings, as contrasted with the white, make the Dutch Cavy very beautiful.

Himalayan

Himalayan, like the Dutch, also derives its name from a rabbit with similar markings. The markings consist of black patches on the nose, feet and ears. The rest of the coat is pure white. The fact that the Himalayan is in good supply and is a very beautiful variety makes him one of the ideal Cavies.

Tortoise-and-White

This is one of the oldest and most popular breeds. It is easy to raise and affords interest in breeding because it is difficult to reproduce true colors.

A good Tortoise-and-White should contain as many black, red and white square-cut patches as possible. These patches should be of equal size and placed alternately upon each side.

Because of the difficulty in breeding the Tortoise-and-White, a perfectly marked specimen can be worth quite a bit of money. Whether you have a grand champion or not, this is one of the most fascinating and beautiful of the Cavies.

3.
Care

Although the Cavy is a native of South America, which differs in climate and altitude from our own, his hardy and robust nature has enabled him to thrive as well here as in his native country. Climate and altitude are not as important to the health of your Cavy as is proper care.

A wild Cavy, showing the natural coloring of the animal in its undomesticated form.

Precautions must be taken to ensure the comfort and health of your Cavy. This does not imply that he should be over-protected or coddled, but like any other animal, a certain measure of care should be exercised.

Himalayan Cavies in outdoor surroundings. Cavies must not be allowed to roam free outside the house.

Housing

Only in the warmer tropical and semi-tropical climates can the Cavy be successfully kept outdoors unprotected all year round. Anywhere else a "hutch" (a box-like pen or house) must be provided. Though there may be a thousand different ways of housing Cavies, certain general rules must be followed.

The most important aspect is not what you put them in, but where you put them. The Cavy must always be in clean, pleasant, sanitary surroundings. It must be kept

Above: This Cavy has had hay provided in its cage.

Right: A female Cavy showing a good head conformation.

23

in mind that Cavies are very sensitive to drafts, moisture and extreme temperatures. Generally, Cavies should not be exposed to temperatures below 60 or above 90°F. More important than the amount of heat is that it remain constant. Care should be taken to have a minimum temperature variation. A grown Cavy can withstand a great deal of cold as long as no draft is present.

Another important factor to consider in the housing of Cavies is the number to be housed and their sex. It is not advisable to keep large number of Cavies in one hutch; six to eight females and one male is the limit. There should never be more than one male at a time in a hutch because when two males are together they will fight. When a male and a number of females are together, females should be removed as soon as they show signs of pregnancy, thereby avoiding the danger of premature birth. After the young have been weaned, the mother can be returned to the hutch with the male.

An Abyssinian mother and her albino baby.

Metal cages with appropriate spacing between the bars are among the best housing units you can provide for your Cavies.Check with your pet dealer to see what is available and recommended—don't let your pets become subject to disease and potential danger by using defective homemade substitutes.

Because Cavies do not climb, jump or gnaw on wood, their houses do not need to be elaborate. They must be cozy, waterproof and ventilated. Since Cavies spend most of their time running around, a large floor space should be provided. This space can be enlarged by utilizing ramps or stairways connecting the floor with an upper level or shelf. This shelf should be about four inches from the floor and in a dark corner. It serves a dual purpose; Cavies like to use it as a perch (in much the same way as birds do), and it provides a kind of nest where they will sleep underneath the shelf. This shelf then serves as a play area leaving the lower level free for nesting and feeding.

Whether you intend to have one or many Cavies, it should be kept in mind that each Cavy requires a minimum of one square foot of floor space and one cubic foot of air space. The dimensions and designs of your hutch will usually be governed by two factors: the number of Cavies you intend to house and the amount of time and money you intend to invest. A wooden box, 24 inches by 12 inches and 12 inches high, is suitable for housing one Cavy. An enclosure 30 inches by 36 inches, 12 to 15 inches high, is large enough for a male and five or six breeding females.

Last, but not least in importance, is that you keep your hutch securely locked so that no dog, cat, or any other animal can get at your pets. The Cavy is not a fighter; he has no means of defense and will offer no resistance to his enemies.

As long as you follow these general rules you are free to design your hutch to your own personal specifications.

This black female shows good solidity of color. Photo by Michael Gilroy.

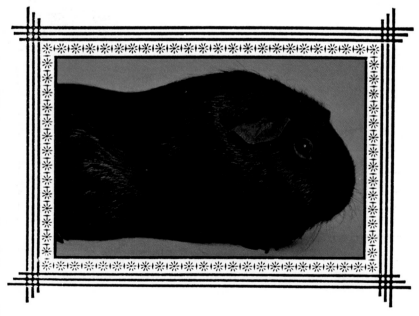

4.
Feeding

The Cavy is a strict vegetarian. His tastes include almost all vegetables and he will eat just about anything you put in front of him. Although he can live on a diet of ordinary lawn clippings, care must be taken to give him a variety of foods to insure his health and good condi-

Alfalfa cubes and Cavy pellets obtainable at pet shops are the mainstays of the diet for your pet.

tion. A good balanced diet will consist of fresh greens, hay, water and salt, supplemented by a commercially prepared pellet or chow.

Training

The Cavy is not known for its intelligence, but for its affection. It is perhaps because of this their training has been limited. The animal is not stupid, but he has a singleness of purpose—to be affectionate and friendly. It seems the Cavy has been trained only to display this purpose. For example, Cavies have been known to sit up and beg and even to whistle in anticipation of the arrival of their masters.

Fresh foods

The only green foods the Cavy does not like are onions, peppers and potatoes. This leaves an immense number of foods that he does like. The following is a list of fresh foods that he likes and are good for him:

Alfalfa (green)	Dandelions
Apples	Lettuce
Cauliflower	Lawn Clippings
Celery Tops	Spinach
Clover (green)	Sugar Beets
Corn (green)	Tomatoes

Many breeders say that it is not good to feed cabbage to Cavies, while an equal number say that it is a healthy food. The best policy in this situation is to feed a small quantity to your pet, and if he likes it, fine; you can continue feeding him cabbage. If, on the other hand, he does not like it, simply do not give him any more. This is a good policy to follow in feeding Cavies all new food. It should be given to them a little at a time until they become accustomed to it. It is important to experiment

This male is a badly marked specimen of the Dalmatian type—but his lack of conformation to the standard for show animals won't prevent him from making an excellent pet. Photo by Michael Gilroy.

with different types of foods to find out what they like and what is good for them.

The fact that most of the fresh foods mentioned are both inexpensive and readily available makes feeding your Cavy a simple matter. In addition, many of these foods are used on your own dinner table making it convenient to share with your pet.

Dry foods

Timothy hay, oats, dry corn, bran, barley meal and dried bread are the common dry foods fed to Cavies. These should be fed especially in the winter months when green foods are scarcer. Timothy hay is by far the most important of these because it can be used first as feed, and, after the seeds and leaves have been consumed by the Cavy, the stems remain to be used by them as bedding.

Oats, bran and dry corn can be mixed or fed separately to great advantage. At least one of the three should be fed to your Cavy every day. Stale bread soaked in milk is a desirable food for mothers with young, as it aids the mother in producing milk.

Commercially prepared foods

Commercially prepared chows or dried pellets formulated especially for Cavies are readily available in pet stores. These should be included with the Cavy's food, following the direction thereon. Your pet must be given water when feeding these prepared foods as they contain no moisture.

A pet cavy won't reach its potential for growth and good looks unless it is cared for properly and fed correctly.

These foods are extremely important in the wintertime because they are fortified with Vitamin C, usually provided by green foods, particularly carrots and lettuce. In order to guarantee the potency of the Vitamin C content, these prepared foods should be stored in a dry place and kept in a closed container.

Water

Cavies can live without water or liquid of any kind if they are fed only on a diet of green vegetables. Water, as we have seen, is necessary when prepared foods are used to supplement the diet. A piece of rock salt should always be available.

Proper feeding methods

Food cups and sanitary water bottles should be suspended from the cage walls in order to prevent contamination by urine and feces. Water should be changed once a day. At each meal, Cavies should be fed just enough to easily finish by the time you next feed them. Cavies should be fed twice a day, morning and evening. However, you can deviate from this and feed them more often. The important thing to remember is that regularity is essential, and that punctuality should be closely observed.

5.
Grooming

A half-teaspoon of linseed or cod-liver oil should be added to the diet daily. This will add greatly to the luster and body of the coat. In the case of show animals, it is advisable to comb and brush the hair every day. This procedure can also be used with your pet to insure a

This Cavy is being groomed for an exhibition. Pet Cavies need not be groomed to perfection, but for their health's sake they must be kept clean. Photo by R. Hanson.

good smooth, lustrous coat. Another simple method is to rub the animal from his nose clear down his back with the palm of your hand. Not only does this do wonders for his coat, but by this treatment he will become more tame and affectionate.

To bathe your Cavies, use a cat shampoo recommended and sold by your pet shop. Follow the manufacturer's instructions and wash the Cavy thoroughly, loosening up all the dirt and stains. Finish up by rinsing the animal in clean water, and then rub and brush the coat until thoroughly dry. This whole operation should be performed in warm surroundings.

On a correctly groomed Peruvian such as the one shown here it is hard to tell the front end from the rear end. Photo by Mrs. I. Rutledge.

6.
Ailments

As we have already noted, the Cavy is a very healthy animal and when properly housed and fed will remain so and thrive quite well without extra precautions. The usual causes of sickness may be a sudden draft, a change in temperature, too much dampness, or simply a broken tooth preventing the Cavy from eating dry foods.

A pet Cavy cannot fend for itself, so its owner must provide it with the good care it deserves.

Alertness and clearness of eye are signs of good health. Photo by Brian Seed.

When Cavies are sick, they usually exhibit one or more of the following symptoms: they sit perfectly still all hunched up; there is a ruffled appearance to the hair around the mouth; the coat is in an untidy or rough condition; they lack appetite; or they lose weight rapidly.

Prevention

If you always try to take good care of your pet, rather than try to cure him when he is sick, you will have little experience with sick Cavies. "An ounce of prevention is worth a pound of cure" is always good to remember.

Suggested safeguards against the outbreak or spread of disease are:

1. Always protect your Cavy from unsanitary conditions.
2. Clean cages at least once a week.
3. Disinfect cages.
4. Feed animals a balanced diet of dry and green foods.
5. Offer fresh drinking water daily in clean containers.
6. Provide adequate space for exercise.
7. Provide adequate light and ventilation.
8. Keep other pets away.
9. Separate any sick Cavies immediately.
10. Keep food free of contamination by rats and mice.
11. (a) Keep males separate.
    (b) Keep pregnant females separate.
12. Do not handle pregnant females too much.
13. Do not overbreed females.
14. Always feed clean fresh foods, *never* frozen foods.

When a sick Cavy is observed, he should be isolated until you find out what ails him and treat him accordingly.

Bronchial troubles

Pneumonia and colds occur when the animal is subjected to cold, dampness, draft and unsanitary conditions. Obviously, it is advisable to protect your pet from such circumstances. A dry husky cough is the symptom of bronchial trouble and, if detected, the animal should be bedded on meadow hay and the air kept at an even temperature, with a boiling kettle or vaporizer nearby so that the air does not become too dry.

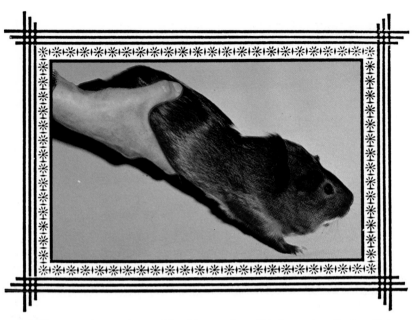

A Cavy won't stay in good health very long if it is continually handled this way—this is one of the WRONG ways to lift a Cavy. Photo by Mrs. I. Rutledge.

Diarrhea

Perhaps the most common ailment but regrettably it is not often discovered until it is too late. It is usually caused by careless feeding (too much green food and not enough dry foods), although it can be the result of a cold. Remedy—leafy greens should be avoided. Consult your veterinarian for recommended treatment.

Indigestion

Usually caused by overfeeding, or lack of proper exercise, or bad ventilation, or insufficient light. The remedy is simple. Again, consult your veterinarian.

Cavies like and benefit from occasional treats of green food, but it's not wise to keep mixing up their diet with new vegetative temptations. Photo by Louise Van der Meid.

Broken teeth

Result from fighting or accidentally bumping into something. If you discover broken teeth you should isolate the animal, feed him soft foods, and in a short time the teeth will grow back.

Wounds

While seldom found, they are the result of fighting. The best treatment is to cut away the surrounding hair, cleanse with lukewarm water, and apply petroleum jelly or zinc ointment.

Eye diseases and injuries

These result from a number of causes. The usual symptom is a watery condition of the eye. Use a pet eyewash or eye cream suitable for cats. In severe cases, professional help is advisable.

Lice, mites, fleas and ticks

Usually found during summer months and result from contact with other pets. These parasites are easily eliminated by dusting or rubbing the Cavy with insecticide powder which is easily obtainable from your petshop. Again, use a cat rather than a dog flea powder. Bedding should be removed and the hutch thoroughly disinfected.

Because the symptoms of these various ailments are similar even a trained person may have difficulty distinguishing one disease from another. If you are ever in doubt about the nature of an ailment do not hesitate to consult a veterinarian.

7.

Breeding

Breeding of Cavies does not present any great difficulty
to the novice. The Cavy is ideally suited for obtaining
results quickly. He offers the amateur as well as professional breeder more opportunities for experimentation
in breeding than does any other animal.

*A mother Cavy and two of her babies; not every Cavy
mother takes good care of her offspring.*

The cavy is a member of the rodent family but it does not follow the normal rodent pattern with regard to bearing its young. It has a very long gestation period for so small an animal, 70 days being the usual time although births a few days before or after are not unusual. Because of this long gestation period the babies are born with their eyes open, fully furred, and able to run around almost immediately. Their stomachs are capable of taking the same food as adults and digesting it without any trouble. It is quite normal to see babies chewing small pieces of hay even before they are dry from birth. The sow can rear four babies, and even more in the summer, from her two milk glands, the babies seeming to wait their turn to be fed although a very tiny baby may be pushed away. Plenty of food for the sow and some bread and milk for the babies will help a large litter to be reared successfully, and provided they are well fed they will grow quite normally once they get past weaning age and will not be stunted as is sometimes supposed.

Below:haphazard matings produce haphazard results;it takes controlled breeding procedures to produce consistency of result such as shown on the facing page.

Young sows can be bred at about 5 months of age provided they are fit and well. Some breeds vary on the recommended age but they should not be left too long before being bred as a sow that has not had a litter by the time she is 10 months old is more likely to have trouble due to her bones and ligaments being less supple and she may prove difficult to mate.

Young boars, although they will behave rather precociously as young as 4 weeks of age, are not usually potent until about 10 weeks but different breeds vary. It does no harm to give a young boar a sow and in fact it will stop him fretting on his own. When he is about 6 months old he is usually large enough to manage quite well with more sows.

A Silver Agouti mother and her nicely colored babies.

Crispness of markings in the multicolored varieties is highly desirable but not always easy to achieve. Photo by Brian Seed.

While four or five sows can be run with one boar you must NEVER have more than one boar in the breeding pen as they would kill one another even if they have been brought up together. Once they have sight and smell of sows they must never again be put with another boar.

Some fanciers prefer leaving the pregnant sows in with the boar and letting them litter in the breeding pen together. Another practice is to remove the pregnant sow from the main breeding pen and put her into a smaller pen some time before birth so that she can have her litter on her own, and yet another method is to have one boar with one sow and to remove the boar shortly before the sow is due to litter. Each method has its advantages and disadvantages which each fancier can evaluate according to circumstances.

The number of babies born is determined by the sow; the boar merely fertilizes the ova released by the sow, and litters of 1 to 4 are usual but litters of 5-10 have been recorded. Four babies is ideally plenty for a sow to rear but in the winter a litter of this size can be a bit of a strain and some help should be given, either by fostering the babies or feeding them.

An albino Cavy; note the red eye.

Most sows will breed up to about 3 years of age although some will stop before this and some will go on until they are 4 or 5, the average life span of a cavy being 3-5 years though here again some individuals will go on to 8 or 9 years. Boars seem to live longer than sows and can sire occasional litters at 5 or even older.

Shorthaired Cavies are of course easier to groom than their longhaired cousins. Photo by Michael Gilroy.

Difficulties Giving Birth

Most sows can give birth quite easily to surprisingly large babies, although sometimes with a first litter there may be a dead one. If there is only one baby which is large it may die during birth if this is prolonged. However, when difficulties do arise there is quite a lot that can be done to help, either by a vet or by an experienced breeder. Luckily it is not often that assistance is required as the cavy is a very good mother and can do all that is necessary herself.

The licking and cleaning of the babies stimulates the sow's contractions for the birth of the next baby and when the last baby is born any afterbirth that has not been passed will come away during the next 12 hours or so; it does not necessarily all come away at once.

Gradual changes take place in the body of the sow and the eating of the afterbirth, or most of it, stimulates chemical changes and the milk starts to flow into the milk glands. This causes the sow to want to suckle, but if the sow at first does not show any interest in the babies and hides in a corner give her something interesting to eat, dry the babies off, and make sure that they are warm. If there is more than one baby they usually keep one another warm, but a single baby could become chilled if the weather is particularly cold so it is best to take it into the house until the sow starts to move about, at which time it can be returned to her and she will soon start fussing over it.

Sometimes a young sow with her first litter will act as if she is frightened of them, particularly if she has had a

There is no escaping the fact that Cavies can be downright cute! Photo by Brian Seed.

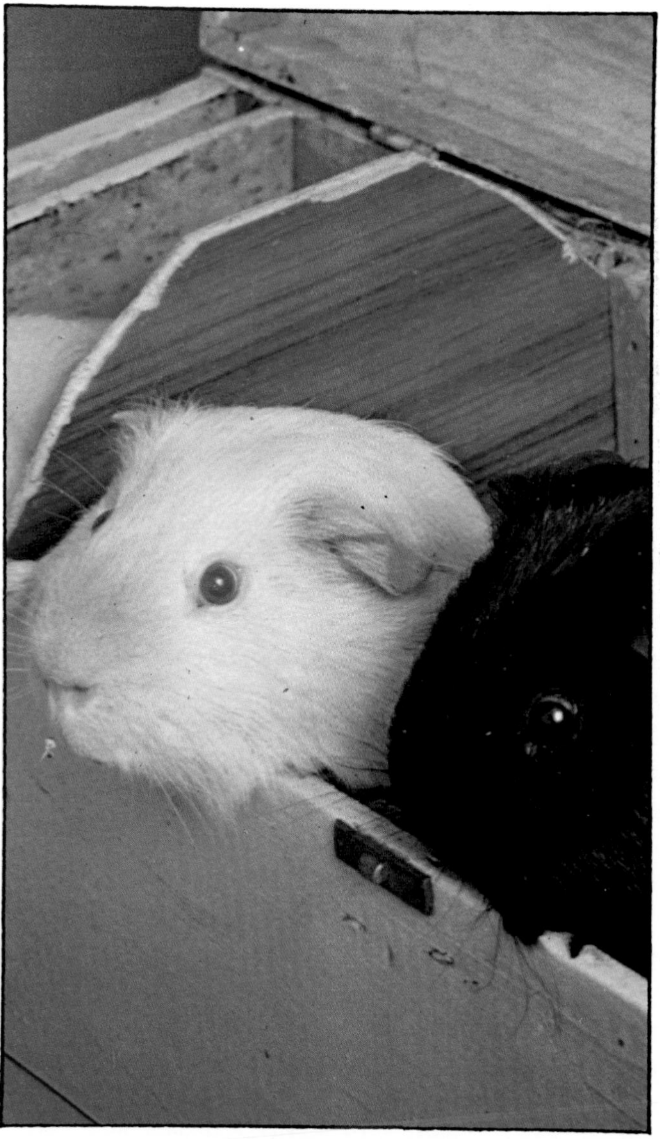

bit of trouble. She will take a look, snort, and run to the farthest corner of the pen. Hanging a cloth over the pen to keep it dark and leaving some interesting food near the babies usually results in the sow adjusting, becoming broody, and starting to take an interest. Once she starts licking them you know she will be all right.

Fostering and Feeding of Babies

Large litters can be split up and given to sows that have only one or two babies for most cavies will happily foster babies. Usually this is most successfully done when the babies are only a few days old as it can be a little more difficult when the foster mother's babies are older than the other babies; the younger ones may get pushed out when it is feeding time. A sow with only one baby makes an ideal foster mother. Rub some of the damp litter from the foster mother around the baby and if the sow starts licking and fussing over it then you can be sure she will accept and feed it. However, if she will not accept it she will keep pushing it away, grind her teeth, and may even make a lunge at the baby, although sows do not usually hurt them. In such cases the baby will have to be returned to its original mother. If a baby is not getting enough milk it usually gets a "tucked up" look over the hips and hind legs. As the new fancier progresses he will recognize this look and be able to ensure that the particular baby is fed extra milk by means of an eye dropper for a few days until it can fight its way to the milk with the others.

If a mother should die and you are left with a litter that you cannot foster, then they can be hand reared. Milk powder can be obtained from most pet shops, and 1 teaspoonful of this mixed with a little warm milk to a creamy consistency that will run through an eye dropper should be fed every two hours for the first day or so.

Cavies appeal to people of all ages—you don't have to be a youngster to enjoy a Cavy.

Young Cavies will grow quickly if given the right care; good nutrition is one of the most important considerations. Photo by Louise Van der Meid.

Ideally this should be through the night also, but one feed would do at night. The babies soon become adept at sucking at the dropper. Do not squeeze the milk into their mouths or they will choke; let them take it at their own pace, about one eye dropper full each at first and increase it to whatever they will take. In addition to this always put some of the mixture mashed with a little wheat bread in a shallow dish so that they can get accustomed to helping themselves. Once they do this keep the dish clean and freshly filled each day and stop the feeding by eye dropper except for perhaps the smaller or slower ones. You will have to clean up the babies around the face and mouth as their mother would normally do this. They will, in addition to the milk, require exactly the same food as an adult cavy, but for the first few days it is wise to mince up the carrot and beets, unless of course it is summer and you can find some succulent grass for them. The time and effort spent in hand rearing is well rewarded by the sense of achievement it gives you, particularly if one turns out in the end to be a big winner or a pretty pet.

Sexing

Sexing young cavies can be a bit of a problem until you are used to doing this; when they are older the difference is quite obvious. They are, however, quite similar while very young. The male will show a tiny round, slightly raised protrusion about the size of a pin head with a tiny dot in the center, and very slight gentle pressure in front of this will usually result in the tiny penis showing slightly, but do not press or poke around the area. The female looks very similar but instead of a tiny round opening from which she urinates it is slightly elongated, more like a tiny slit, and below this the division of the vagina and the anal opening may show slightly as a tiny pink blob of flesh; but again do not

Himalayan Cavies are solid white when born; the second color develops later on. Photo by R. Hanson.

poke or prod about the area; close examination of an actual cavy will show a slight difference and practice will soon make it quite easy. Young boars will usually demonstrate their sex even while with their mother by walking on their toes and weaving their bodies about and making a familiar purring noise. If a young weaner is put with a strange young cavy it will quickly demonstrate if it is male or female. The male will behave as previously described but a young female will just look around or look rather timid. Adopt this method only if you cannot determine the sex by the former method as your youngster could be severely told off by the strange cavy. The first minute or so should give you an indication before any aggression sets in.

Young cavies should be handled with care as they are inclined to jump about and can even jump right out of the pen if a good deep drop board is not used. When handling them they should be handled as the adults with the hand underneath the belly and the hind legs not able to get a foothold, thus preventing them from jumping. Both hands should be employed for handling youngsters, one supporting and the other over the top of them. They will throw themselves right out of your hands if care is not taken and severely injure or kill themselves.

Breeding Records

If you are keeping and breeding cavies with showing in mind, records should be kept of each animal that you intend to breed or show. On this record should be entered details of their own breeding if this is obtainable from your original supplier, details of the animal's markings or make-up, its date of birth and, if you keep more than one breed, its breed and from what strain or breeder it came.

Keeping details of their litters and what they have produced and what similar characteristics they appear to pass on to their offspring when mated to different animals is also recommended. These details can in future generations often prove helpful, especially when mating related animals together or in showing that it would **not** be wise to mate certain individuals together because of inherited characteristics that you do not want to increase in your stock.

Breeders of Cavies have personal preferences as to the different color varieties they want to deal with; the boar shown here is a Self Red.

If the animal is a show cavy or a potential one then records of its progress, its placings at shows, comments on points that any particular judge seemed to prefer, the competition, and so on, can again prove to be quite helpful in the future, particularly if showing again under the same judge. Some studs have cards placed on the pens on which details are entered.

Cavies like and can benefit from carrots—provided the carrots are fresh and clean and not fed too often. Photo by Tom Caravaglia.

8.
Showing

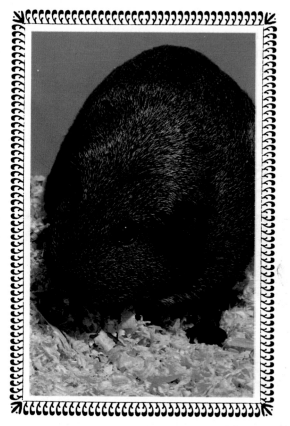

Each year, large poultry and pet stock exhibitions are held in various parts of the country. It is only through exhibiting that a breeder really learns the quality of his Cavies. By attending these shows you can learn and appreciate what good stock is. It is interesting to compare stock and learn why one Cavy is better than another.

Cleanliness is an important consideration in a show animal. Photo by Michael Gilroy.

These Cavies are being judged at a show in Scotland—some of the finest Cavies in the world are bred in the United Kingdom.

Cash prizes are awarded in many different classes in these large shows. More important than this is that a breeder becomes nationally known if he exhibits high quality stock. Many sales are usually made in the show-room by breeders who have stock on exhibition, and extravagant prices are received for exhibition stock.

The smaller local or community shows should not be overlooked because they bring local breeders and fanciers together, affording an excellent opportunity to get acquainted with the older breeders and acquire not only valuable information but new and interesting friends.

9.
Conclusion

The Cavy is easy to care for, and with proper care he will live to be over seven years old. The amount of care required is so small that young children are able to take full responsibility for them, thereby deriving a great deal of pleasure and satisfaction.

Cavies are not the smartest animals in the world, but they respond with affection to attention and good care. Photo by Brian Seed.

He does not scratch or bite; he is a poor climber and does not jump. Placed on a table top, barring an accident, he will remain there, just as he will remain in an open top box.

His small size makes the Cavy ideal for the city. He can be housed easily and cheaply in almost any location. He will eat small amounts of readily available inexpensive food.

He is affectionate and gentle in manner. He is known for his cleanliness.

Because it is so simple to produce the many breeds and varieties of Cavies many people breed Cavies as a hobby. The relaxation offered by this hobby provides a pleasant diversion from the daily routine of life.

No matter whether you are a man, woman or child, or whether you are interested in him as a pet or as a potential breeder, the Cavy certainly offers you a great experience.